GEORGE MICHAEL

YOU HAVE BEEN LOVED

Written by

Carolyn Thomas

BOOKS

First Published Danann Publishing Ltd 2019

WARNING: For private domestic use only, any unauthorised Copying, hiring, lending or public performance of this book is illegal.

CAT NO: DAN0340

Photography courtesy of

Getty images:

Kevin Winter	Diana Scrimgeour/Redferns
Eddy Lemaistre/Corbis	Brian Rasic
FG/Bauer-Griffin	Dave Hogan/Live 8
Pete Cronin/Redferns	Morena Brengola
John Rogers/Daily Express/Hulton Archive	Odd Andersen/AFP
Pete Still/Redferns	Samuel Kubani/AFP
Ian Dickson/Redferns	Evert Elzinga/AFP
Michael Putland	Dave J Hogan
Georges De Keerle	Mondadori Portfolio
Rob Verhorst/Redferns	rune hellestad/Corbis
Mick Hutson/Redferns	Chris Grieve/Daily Mirror/Mirrorpix
Steve Rapport/Photoshot	Pascal Le Segretain

Book layout & design Darren Grice at Ctrl-d

Made in EU.

ISBN: 978-1-9997050-5-3

CONTENTS

INTRODUCTION

George Michael is one of the most successful British musical artists of all time.

After rising to fame in the pop duo Wham! in the early 1980s, George went on to have a hugely successful international solo career as a singer, writer, producer and performer.

He clocked up 11 number one hits in the UK alone and sold more than 100m albums worldwide during a career spanning almost four decades. As the creator of infectiously catchy pop songs with Wham! and then more reflective and soulful tracks as a mature solo artist, he became a superstar throughout the world, winning armfuls of prestigious awards and millions of fans.

Yet running alongside this phenomenal success, George had a self-destructive streak. Despite being a pin up for teenage girls, he was a troubled soul; a gay man who hid his true sexuality for years and consequently endured endless press speculation about his love life. Struggling to come to terms with losing his first love and his mother within a few years of each other, George suffered episodes of depression, drug addiction, headline-making arrests and a famous legal battle with his record company.

Yet through all his difficulties, his talent never let him down. And nor did his legions of loyal fans who were distraught over his sudden death on Christmas Day 2016, aged just 53.

THIS IS HIS STORY ....

8

1963 - 1979

I KNEW YOU WERE WAITING FOR ME

It's crazy but true that the world might have missed out on the genius of George Michael had he not banged his head as a child.

For Britain's biggest pop star of the 1980s was not from a musical family and had no other explanation for his precocious and extraordinary talent.

As a little boy, George was obsessed with insects and creepy-crawlies, often getting up early in the morning to go out and collect them. But aged eight he developed an interest in music, which he subsequently attributed to having suffered a bang on the head. 'I know it sounds bizarre and unlikely, but it was quite a bang and [after it] all my interests changed, everything changed in six months. Suddenly, all I wanted to know about was music. It just seemed a very, very strange thing. And I have a theory that maybe it was something to do with this accident, this whole left-brain, right-brain thing. Nobody in my family seemed to notice but I became absolutely obsessed with music and everything changed after that.'

George Michael was born Georgios Kyriacos Panayiotou on 25 June 1963 into a first-generation Greek Cypriot family living in Finchley, North London.

His father, Kyriacos, had come to the UK from Cyprus in the early 1950s and filled with immigrant zeal and commitment to better himself, worked hard to improve his lot in life. He

changed his name to Jack Panos for ease of integration and began work in the restaurant trade, initially as a waiter.

Jack married an English dancer called Lesley Angold, a kind and friendly girl who, although ostensibly from a working-class background, had attended a convent school and spoke with a middle-class accent. George picked up her way of speaking, so that people were often surprised to meet his father. Years later George discovered that his roots were Jewish on his mother's side. Lesley's wealthy Victorian grandmother had disowned her daughter (Lesley's mother) for marrying a 'gentile'. George always maintained that Lesley had inherited a slightly Victorian mentality and had an odd relationship with money, being slightly suspicious of it and not convinced that it brought happiness. Although she worked hard to support her family she did not have the same drive and interest in upward social mobility as her go-getting, highly ambitious husband. 'Being half my mother and half my father genetically was never going to be easy', George said subsequently.

However, George was very close to his mother until the day she died. They looked alike and shared many character traits. Lesley was always his biggest supporter and believed in him when others didn't.

Overall George had a happy childhood, though his accounts

of his early life varied over the years. As the youngest child and a much longed-for son he spoke of being indulged by his parents and two older sisters Melanie and Yioda, and of being aware of the privileges he was afforded merely because he was a boy in the Greek Cypriot patriarchal culture. He has described feeling guilty about the fact that he could 'get away' with almost anything and generally had an easier ride than his older sisters.

A childhood present of a tape recorder was put to good use as George began to write songs and record them. He and his sisters had plenty of time to pursue their own interests while both their parents worked hard to improve their lot. Lesley worked outside the house as well as bringing up her three children and keeping the house spotless. One of her jobs was in a fish and chip shop – something she hated because of the way the smell of fish lingered in her hair.

Jack had worked his way up from waiting tables to restaurant manager and then eventually opening his own restaurant, Mr Jack's, where a young George was also expected to help out – often his job was washing up.

In an interview with Rolling Stone magazine, George remembered that his parents were 'just constantly exhausted. They were both working so hard to get us where they wanted us to but that made them authoritarian. It was a chilly home where I was never praised, never held. So it was not exactly the Little House on the Prairie. It really wasn't.'

By 1975 Jack's restaurant was doing so well that the family was able to move from their flat above a launderette in London to the more up-market suburb of Radlett, in Hertfordshire. Aged 12, George was enrolled at Bushey Meads secondary school, where a life-changing meeting took place. For it was in a classroom at Bushey Meads that George met the boy who was to become so important to his story, Andrew Ridgeley,

who went on to become the other half of pop duo Wham!

Their friendship began when Andrew put up his hand to offer to help settle in the new boy George, nicknamed Yog, a diminutive resulting from the Greek pronunciation of his name. The two boys hit it off immediately. They had plenty in common, including a mixed heritage family background; Andrew's father being of Italian and Egyptian descent, while his mother was Scottish. And of course both boys were huge music fans.

At the start of their friendship, Andrew seemed to have the upper hand. He was everything that George was not – the school's cool cat, good-looking, confident, funny and popular. George was a later developer so as a 12-year-old was still carrying puppy fat, wearing huge glasses and struggling with bad skin and a monobrow. Nevertheless the two of them connected and quickly became inseparable teenagers. George always had a great sense of humour and the pair of them were always laughing and larking about.

'Oh, the press loved all those stories about me being an ugly duckling, but they overplayed them,' said George in a 1986 interview with Number 1 magazine. 'From the physical point of view of Andrew being a great dresser and me being the short, fat, spotty one with glasses, that is all true, basically because I never bothered looking in the mirror until I was about 13. But the pair of us were always very loud, I wasn't at all introverted. At 16 I was a pretty confident boy with girls and most things. If I look back at myself when I was 13 or 14 – I'd have been very offended if I'd heard people say I was all those dreadful things!'

Before long both boys began writing songs together. Elton John, Queen and David Bowie were all big influences on their early work. George actually began his personal album collection with a copy of Elton John's 1974 album Caribou. Little did George know it when he listened to the album in his bedroom that he would go on to duet with Elton to one of the

tracks on this album, Don't let the Sun Go Down On Me.

Having decided that academia wouldn't get them where they wanted to be George and Andrew left school to try their luck as pop stars.

This led to great tension in the Panayiotou family. George's father did not have a musical bone in his body and was horrified to learn that his son's interest and ambitions centred on the music industry – he didn't even consider that George had an especially good voice. Perhaps unsurprisingly he thought his son's dream of becoming a famous pop star was pie in the sky. Having worked so hard himself to move from his homeland to the UK to improve his family's fortunes, he thought that George was now wasting his life chances. He expected his son to do as he was told and continue his education and then take on a more traditional line of employment.

But George wouldn't have any of it. He was dead set on being a musician. It was the first time he had really stood up to his father in any way. But he was now 16 and determined he wasn't staying on at school.

After some tussling his disappointed father gave up trying to dissuade him, shrugged his shoulders and seemingly wrote him off.

'I think all hopes for my academic future were crumbled, you know, so it was pretty tough at the beginning, they [his parents] weren't happy,' said George in an interview with Capital Radio in 1998. But he'd got his way, escaped parental expectations and swerved further schooling.

HIS WORLD SEEMED FULL OF
EXCITING POSSIBILITIES.

12

Wham during the recording of Club Tropicana at Pikes
Hotel in Ibiza on May 16, 1983

1 9 8 0 – 1 9 8 3

YOUNG GUNS GO
FOR IT

The immediate reality was not glamorous – George and Andrew did a mixture of humdrum jobs and sometimes signed on the dole, while busking and trying their luck in various music groups. George also worked as a DJ in local small-time venues and as a part time cinema attendant.

Having got into soul music, George and Andrew enjoyed spending their evenings in clubs and discos. Then two different musical genres became popular in the late 1970s – punk and ska.

Punk held little attraction for the pair, but ska music did resonate with them.

Originally a fusion of traditional Jamaican music with American R&B, ska enjoyed a revival in the UK in the late 70s/early 80s, this time taking the form of '2-Tone', popularised by bands such as The Specials and Madness.

It influenced George and Andrew so that their first serious musical venture was the formation of a ska band called The Executive , its members also included Andrew's brother Paul and two school friends Andrew Leaver and David Mortimer (later known as David Austin, who remained a lifelong friend and George's some-time manager).

Although it enjoyed some success locally, The Executive was short-lived and when it eventually fell apart Andrew and George decided to go ahead as a duo. They recorded

a home-made tape, about 10 minutes long and trekked around various record companies trying to drum up interest. With the confidence of youth they used to walk into record company offices and swear blind that they had appointments – reckoning that the tactic meant they got into see somebody at least 50% of the time.

Despite this tape including early versions of songs which went on to be monster hits - Wham Rap! (Enjoy What You Do?), Club Tropicana, Come On! and Careless Whisper - it was initially rejected by all the major labels.

It was around this time that schoolfriend and Andrew's then girlfriend Shirlie Holliman, became involved. Shirlie was later famous in her own right as Wham!'s backing singer and dancer and later one half of another duo, Pepsi and Shirlie. But initially she was in it for fun and she, George and Andrew became well-known locally by choreographing and performing dance routines at local nightclubs.

'I'd been friends with George and Andrew since school - I was the year above them,' Shirlie recalls. 'George used to make up all these dance routines which we'd do in nightclubs; we were either great or so bad that everybody cleared the floor. Wham! started out as an extension of the dance routines. George was the organiser, Andrew had all the charisma.'

George was the main songwriter and his musical talent and contribution was evidently greater than Andrew's. But without his best friend by his side, it seems unlikely George would have had the guts or the image to forge ahead with a career as a pop star.

Andrew was the perfect foil for George yet was to suffer over the years as critics questioned the exact nature of his role in the band – but he undoubtedly gave Wham its style and early appeal. George often spoke of how influenced he was by his friend, including in an interview with Rolling Stone magazine when he said; 'His clothes were always perfect, he was really stylish, all the girls liked him. And that was something that I always wanted to be, because I was such a mess to look at. The whole idea of being a physically attractive personality never really occurred to me until I met him'.

Andrew was also a huge emotional support for George. And above all, the two of them as real friends had such enormous fun getting into all sorts of scrapes and having a good time. Although both boys were huge music fans there is no doubt that they also wanted to be famous. While for some musicians fame is an unwelcome by-product of their passion – for George and Andrew it was part of the ambition, although ironically George was eventually to discover that fame wasn't what he wanted after all.

But in the early days at least George was certain that he wanted to be a pop star. 'Yeah, I definitely wanted the glory big time' he said, speaking to Capital Radio DJ Neil Fox in 1998. 'I wanted to be a pop star. I started out playing the drums but gathered somewhere along the way that the drummer ends up sitting at the back all the time. I think probably by the time I was about 16 I decided I wanted to be a singer, but all I knew before then was I wanted to write music and be successful with it'.

Eventually the boys struck lucky. After months of hawking around their home-made tape, a local A&R man, Mark Dean who had discovered Soft Cell and ABC offered them a deal. George and Andrew snapped up the offer and signed with

his label Innervision in the spring of 1982. The boys then professionally recorded the four tracks from their demo tape along with a fifth track called Young Guns (Go For It!).

Once George had a foot in the door like this, no one was going to get him out.

He was now a tall and handsome young man, and although Andrew was still considered the cute and charismatic one, George had reinvented himself. Georgios Panayiotou had become, professionally, George Michael and in this new incarnation had lost the spots and the glasses, slimmed down and tamed his curly hair.

Having perfected his image and polished the songs, their next move was to pick a name. They chose Wham! taking it from their debut song, Wham Rap! (Enjoy What You Do) which opened with the lyric; 'Wham! Bam! I am! A man! Job or no job, You can't tell me that I'm not'.

Finally they added to their number by engaging Shirlie and a session singer called Dee C. Lee as backing singer/dancers. The girls were never officially part of Wham! but were a big part of their performances and success.

Wham Rap! - a song mockingly admiring the pair's recent period of unemployment - was released in June 1982. Rap was a relatively new concept in music at that time which helped the track make a great first impression and become a club hit. Stories abound that because of the rap and the soul element of the song, some industry professionals believed the track to be the work of a hot new act from America before setting eyes on George and Andrew.

The fact that the boys already had a following from their days performing dance routines in clubs began to pay off. The band toured their former haunts to promote Wham Rap! It

15

16

was hard work, sometimes they went to half a dozen clubs in one night, but the sight of George and Andrew, bare-chested beneath their leather jackets, cavorting around the two girls was memorable to say the least. They got a great reaction from audiences, becoming more confident with every show.

Useful though this was as practice for live professional performances, the club tour didn't do much for actual sales and the track only reached number 105 in the UK.
It was while performing their second single, Young Guns (Go For It!), at one of London's most famous clubs, Stringfellows that things took off and Wham! got its break. Someone from the BBC spotted the band and invited them to appear on Saturday Superstore – a new Saturday morning BBC children's programme. The appearance went so well that when an act pulled out of a Top Of The Pops performance at the last minute a few weeks later, Wham! was at the forefront of BBC booker's minds and won the coveted slot for themselves.

So on November 4, 1982, Wham! performed Young Guns (Go For It) – a celebration of single life – and, boosted by their knockout performance on the programme, it became their first hit. The obvious chemistry between George and Andrew, coupled with a joyous dance routine, made them a standout act on the show. George had blossomed and dominated the performance dressed in light blue cropped jeans and a leather sleeveless jacket. He took the part of a confident guy berating his friend Andrew's character ('Hey Sucker') for wanting to settle down for 'death by matrimony' as the song's chorus put it.

The record company quickly capitalised on this success by re-releasing Wham Rap! (Enjoy What You Do) and this time it got to number eight in the charts. This was followed by Bad Boys, a story of teenage rebellion, the video for which again depicted George, doing all the singing, as the disrupting influence on Andrew who provided the eye candy. But George was coming into his own as far as the legions of girl fans were concerned – after all, as the Bad Boys lyrics put it, he was now 'nineteen ... handsome, tall and strong'.

Following the arrival of MTV (the music television channel) in 1981, an act's image was more important than ever before. Videos were an essential accompaniment to any release and Wham! did not disappoint. Their videos told a story and the two good looking young boys, came over well on film.

Their music was perfect for the early years of the 1980s. Despite the fact that the UK was experiencing record high unemployment - a topic George frequently referenced in his songs- there was also an upbeat vibe in London and the southeast where materialism and consumerism were the new watchwords.

Pop music duos were popular in the 1980s – think Pet Shop Boys, Tears for Fears, Eurythmics and Soft Cell - but George and Andrew still offered something unique. They were so young – still under 20 when they broke through, yet their long friendship gave the impression of a long-established act. They were cheeky and irreverent – on and off stage – gaining not entirely unwelcome newspaper and magazine coverage with their antics including falling out of clubs. Andrew in particular, gained attention in this area, leading the tabloids to nickname him Animal Andy. To all intents and purposes they appeared as two young guys having a good time, picking up girls and goofing around. Life seemed great fun in Wham!-world as the tanned twosome larked about dressed for perpetual summer in shorts and espadrilles.

George Michael performing with Wham! 1983

But the George Michael of Wham! was to some extent an act - a creation based on Andrew. As quoted by Rolling Stone in 1988 George said; 'I created a man - in the image of a great friend - that the world could love if they chose to, someone who could realise my dreams and make me a star. I called him George Michael, and for almost a decade, he worked his arse off for me, and did as he was told. He was very good at his job, perhaps a little too good.'

The band's fourth single, Club Tropicana was something of a departure – rather than depicting rebellion and revelling in being on the dole, George wrote something very different. Club Tropicana was a catchy number showing beautiful people living it up at a swanky holiday resort – where the drinks were famously free. The twist in the tale was that the end showed that George, Andrew, Shirlie and Dee were actually cabin crew on a break from work. It was released in July 1983 and peaked at number four in the UK, going on to be the 39th best-selling single of that year.

With four UK Top 10 singles to their name Wham! was now a pop phenomenon and released its first album, modestly entitled Fantastic on July 9, 1983. This powerful and confident debut album was a collection of feelgood, frothy tunes. It received mixed reviews, but was a commercial smash, going straight to number one in the UK and spending 113 weeks in the Top 100.

As well as the four successful singles, the album included a reprise of Come On! from their original demo, two new songs (A Ray of Sunshine and Nothing Looks The Same In The Light) and a cover of The Miracles' Love Machine.

This album is however notable for the absence of one song

in particular; Careless Whisper - co-written when the boys were just 17 - was thought at the time not to fit in, song-wise or image-wise.

Because it went on to be a massive hit for George after he'd launched his solo career, Andrew's part in the hit is often forgotten. But he was credited as co-writer and it was definitely something they worked on as a pair in Wham! days.

So despite his father's misgivings, George had made it aged just 20, He was a successful singer, songwriter, producer and arranger of catchy tunes which fizzed with energy and youthful spirit. Yet despite the fact that Fantastic, brought Wham! almost instant success, the boys did not make their fortune from it. The contract with Innervision meant that they were on just £40 a week – better than the dole, but not much.

In his authorised biography Bare, George recalls; '......it was getting ridiculous to have no money, to have to keep asking for a little bit of money for clothes and stuff, when you know how much you are making for other people.'

So in what was famously not to be his only contract dispute with a record company, George resolved to get out of the deal. While the legalities were being thrashed out, Innervision released a medley of tracks from the Fantastic album, which had not been previously available as singles. This put Wham! in the rather unusual position of exhorting fans not to buy that particular record, called Club Fantastic Megamix. 'We don't approve of it and we don't feel that we can recommend that anybody should buy it,' said George and Andrew in a press statement. 'In fact, we would be very unhappy to think that any of our fans might waste their money on it.'

18

19

George Michael and Andrew Ridgeley of Wham
performing at the Lyceum Theatre during the Club
Fantastic Tour, London, UK, 15th November 1983

In the meantime he and Andrew set off on their debut tour, called 'Club Fantastic' in October and November of 1983. All 32 dates sold out and the concerts succeeded in raising the band's profile and cementing their great relationship with fans, comprising mainly adoring young girls. It was sponsored by Fila sportswear and the boys wore those clothes for their performances.

Famously shoving shuttlecocks down their shorts, the pair would often end the shows by taking them out and whacking them into the audience. The link with sportswear was inspired. An aerobics craze had grabbed the UK, inspired by American dance movies Fame and Flashdance, while Jane Fonda workout videos fuelled the movement and even breakfast television had its Green Goddess exhorting the nation to begin the day with a few sit-ups and lunges.

By now Dee C. Lee had tired of life in the background and left the group to join The Style Council. She was replaced by Pepsi DeMacque.

'The tour was chaos,' remembers Shirlie. 'All these screaming fans wanting to get in with George and Andrew. They'd ask Pepsi and I to pass on messages for them with their phone numbers and underwear attached.' This was just the start of a relationship with loyal fans that would last George's entire life.

HIS FANBASE IS ONE OF THE MOST LOYAL AND FORGIVING IN POP HISTORY.

George Michael performing at the Lyceum Theatre during the Club Fantastic Tour, London, UK, 1983

23

George Michael & Andrew Ridgeley performing
at the Hammersmith Odeon, 28 October, 1983

27

George Michael & Andrew Ridgeley performing with Pepsi & Shirlie, 1 October, 1983

1984 - 1986
MAKING IT BIG

After the tour Wham! won their battle to leave Innervision, who settled out of court, and signed with Epic records. They immediately began work on a follow-up album. Leaving nobody in any doubt about their continuing ambition, this was boldly entitled Make it Big and released in October 1984.

This album was the jewel in the crown of Wham!'s output – one review described it as 'almost faultless' and it did indeed see them make it big and conquer America. The album was more successful than their wildest dreams, topping the charts in the UK and the USA. George had developed and improved as a songwriter and also worked as solo producer on this record, incorporating a great sound using soul trumpets, strong bass and harmonies, rather than following the '80s fad for synthesised music. It was an improvement on their previous album in every respect. For several months between 1984 and 1985 Wham was the biggest band in the world – thanks mainly to the incredibly successful album track, released as a single, Wake Me Up Before You Go Go.

The story goes that George was inspired to write this song by a note he saw that Andrew had left his parents, asking for a wake-up call. Having accidentally written 'wake me up, up, before you go ..' he purposely repeated the word 'go' again at the end.

Wake Me Up Before You Go-Go, credited as being written and produced by George, was the big hit on this album, first released as a single in May. It became their first UK and US number one hit and went Platinum in the US, for sales (at that time) of over two million copies.

The accompanying video showed George and Andrew wearing oversized white t-shirts emblazoned with the 'CHOOSE LIFE' slogan in black capital letters, building on a craze for political messages on t-shirts.

Although Make It Big is a short album of just eight tracks, when you realise that among those tracks are Everything She Wants, Freedom and of course the richly seductive, saxophone-led, 'Careless Whisper', it's easy to see why it made its mark.

Careless Whisper was released as a George Michael solo single – the first signal that George had ambitions outside the band.

Now a classic which has topped the charts in 25 countries and sold over six million copies around the world, it features one of the most famous sax solos in popular music.

The song was co-written by George and Andrew when they were just 17 and can't have known much about the dark emotions of which they wrote. It is said to be based on the experiences of a 16-year-old George who two-timed a couple of schoolgirls. In a 2009 interview with the Big Issue magazine, George said he was puzzled about why the song made such an impression on people.

'Is it because so many people have cheated on their partners?' he mused. 'Is that why they connect with it? I have no idea, but it's ironic that this song - which has come to define me in some way - should have been written right at the beginning of my career when I was still so young. I was only 17 and didn't really know much about anything - and certainly nothing much about relationships.'

But then the lyrics have always been secondary to the melody in George Michael compositions. He explained in a 1985 interview that he mainly composed in his head.

'I wrote all the melody lines to 'Careless Whisper' just sitting on a bus. I always write things in my head, let them go around in my head, then I forget about them. Later I come back to them and if the ideas are still there I know that they are commercial and that I like them.

'When I first got a record contract I bought all the equipment that I thought I should use, but when I looked back later at 'Fantastic' I realised that all the best tracks were the ones that I had made up in my head, so I went back to that for the new album. I would hum the melody lines and the bass lines to myself again and again and then once they were cemented in my mind and I knew them off by heart I would go down to the studio with the musicians, get them to play the songs on the keyboards or the bass, telling them the feel that I wanted, and then I'd fill it all in after that'.

Although both Wham! boys were teenage pinups, famous all around the world, George was beginning to eclipse Andrew as far as fans were concerned. Andrew played guitar and had his own adoring fans, but for all intents and purposes this was George Michael's show. As singer, composer and face of the group, he became the bigger draw. He had natural stage presence, so that all eyes were on him.

However, Simon Napier-Bell who was Wham!'s manager between 1983 and 1986, is keen to credit Andrew for his part in the band's success, saying that he played an integral role in giving Wham! its young fun and carefree image.

'Andrew was the image,' he told Classic Pop Magazine. 'Wham! was two lads around town – heterosexual and having fun. George invented the image of the band from observing Andrew. He then chose to act out the role of the second of the two lads around town. Sure, George wrote the songs, but songwriters can be hired or recruited - the one essential of any group is its personality; its image. And that was pure Andrew. Without him, Wham! could never have existed'.

For what the band's adoring female fans did not know was that George was not heterosexual. He was rather more complicated and conflicted about his sexuality. George had had a few girlfriends and sexual experiences with women, but for a few years now had identified as bi-sexual and then came to acknowledge that in fact he was gay. He came out to close friends and one of his sisters when he was just 19 but was persuaded not to tell his parents.

It was not easy to be a gay man in the 1980s, not only were attitudes different then, but also the spectre of AIDS loomed large. This 'acquired immune deficiency syndrome' was a killer at that time and of particular concern to the gay community as it ravaged their number. George said that he was not prepared to worry his parents by bringing AIDS into their lives. Any such admission of non-heterosexuality could also have meant professional suicide for Wham!

Although George said later that he hated the idea that he was a 'fake Andrew' during the Wham! years, he was certainly acting out a persona which undoubtedly came more naturally to his friend.

Looking back at his memories of the Wham! years in a 1997 interview with Hello magazine, Andrew said; 'It's certainly true that, out of the two of us, I was perceived more as the glamorous one. But I think a lot of that was just the media needing to make a distinction between the two of us - me as

29

the pretty-boy sex-symbol and George as the hard-working, talented one'.

Those issues aside, 1984 was an amazing year for the band; topped off with a seasonal hit which has endured ever since, Last Christmas. It was released in December on a double A side with Everything She Wants, written and produced by George. It looked all set to be the Christmas number one – until Band Aid came along – a supergroup formed specially to raise money for that year's Ethiopian famine disaster with their recording of Do They Know it's Christmas.

It was deservedly a huge hit and of course made number one that year, consigning Last Christmas to the number two spot and a note in the pop history books as one of the best-selling singles ever to miss out on the top spot. Last Christmas stayed at number two for five weeks and has made regular re-entries to the UK charts for years since.

In one of the first of his many philanthropic acts, George not only supported the Band Aid single, singing the opening line of the second verse, but then he and Andrew donated all the royalties from Last Christmas to the same charity.

George's involvement meant that by the age of 21 he had made number one in the UK as a part of his own band, a charity band and as a solo artist. He was a major star with more money and success than his father could ever have imagined. Later George said; 'For a while it's magical, you are with your best mate, playing out your fantasies'.

Continuing their pop domination in the mid-80s, Wham! became the first ever Western pop group to perform in China which was just opening up to the outside world following its Cultural Revolution.

Wham!'s gigs were set up as part of an effort to improve friendly relations between China and the West. It was a hotly contested honour, with Queen and the Rolling Stones among the other big names keen to undertake the tour, but Wham!'s manager Simon Napier-Bell won the day for them. Wham! made the 10-day visit to China in March 1985, stopping off during their four-month long 'The Big Tour' which ran from December 1984 until April 1985 comprising 39 shows across the UK, Ireland, Japan, Australia and the United States.

The Chinese dates kicked off with a concert at the Peoples' Gymnasium in Beijing in front of a 12,000-strong crowd. Wham!'s visit to China attracted huge media attention across the world and astounded the Chinese audiences which had ever seen anything like that before, having been used to people in their country standing still when they performed. So the movement and loud, very different music made an incredible impression and was captured in a documentary film about the visit 'Wham! in China: Foreign Skies'.

In 1985 George received his first major solo accolade – the Ivor Novello award for Songwriter of the Year. It was presented to him by his childhood hero Elton John, who described George as, 'The greatest songwriter of his generation...... He deserves to win this award,' Elton continued, '... and I'd like to work with him in the future.'

The did indeed work together, most memorably at another concert which would go into the pop history books. Following up on the successful Band Aid single, Bob Geldof arranged

Andrew Ridgeley and George Michael of Wham! performing together during the 1985 world tour, January 1985

32

Portraits of George Michael of Wham!, Sydney, Australia,
January 1985

George Michael, Bono, Paul McCartney, Freddie Mercury and Bob Geldof perform on stage during the Live Aid concert at Wembley Stadium on 13 July, 1985

LIVE AID

36

Andrew Ridgeley and George Michael of Wham!
perform on stage at Sydney Entertainment
Centre, Sydney, Australia, 27th January 1985

the Live Aid charity concert in July 1985. Keen to support the cause again, George said he would like to take part and memorably sang Don't Let the Sun Go Down on Me with Elton John, while Andrew joined Kiki Dee in back-up vocals. This pop duet has since gone down as one of the best of all time. Six years later, George Michael's Cover to Cover tour regularly included the song, and for the final show at Wembley Arena on March 23 1991, he brought out Elton as a surprise guest to sing it with him. The moment when George announces; 'Ladies and gentlemen Mr Elton John' brings the house down and is a spine-chilling moment even on the recording.

The live recording of this song was released as a single later that year and was a number one hit in both the UK and US.

Having grown up listening to Elton's music, going on to perform and record with him to such universal acclaim was a huge high for George. He contributed vocals to two songs on Elton's, Ice On Fire, Nikita (a UK number three) and Wrap Her Up. The promotional video for Wrap Her Up included footage of George performing on stage with Elton and his band.

George also worked with 70s teen idol David Cassidy, providing backing vocals on his 1985 comeback single The Last Kiss. Once a huge heartthrob himself, David had bestrode the British charts in the 1970s with a run of hit singles and attracted a huge fan base. George remembered being influenced b   y David after watching a film of him in slow motion, heading a ball on top of the London Weekend Television building in London. There were thousands of screaming fans on the ground beneath him, but they couldn't get to him. So George, with that strong image in his mind, wanted to combine his longing for fame with a strong, desire for safety.

They shared a musical publisher in Dick Leahy who arranged a meeting between the pair and George went on to interview David for an article in fashion magazine 'Ritz'. In the intro George explains; 'I was having a particularly hard time coming to terms with my own position in the public eye. I was also keen to find out how a man introduced to this ridiculous [music] business at the tender age of 18 and subject to all its distortions for a solid six years, had actually retained his sanity'

Despite David Cassidy's advice, staying sane and balanced was to be something George would struggle with his whole life. He had already realised that it would be difficult to make the concept that was Wham! work into adulthood. His own tastes had moved on too and he was eager to explore a more grown up sound. Wham! was about being young and in a band and, in that sense, it was limited if they didn't want to be fake and formulaic. They weren't 18 anymore. George's ambitions were taking him onwards and Wham! wasn't going to go with him. Andrew was also missing being able to have anything approaching a proper private life, so without any rancour or arguments the pair agreed to wind Wham! up and go their separate ways. 'After four years of writing, touring and promoting our music around the world I had had enough, said George. 'I realised I was miserable, I had everything I had wanted, but the gap was still there – the circus of it all was distressing'.

So, after five years together Wham! announced its break up to devastated fans in February 1986. By the time they finished, Wham! had become one of the most commercially successful pop acts of the decade with sales of around 28 million albums and 15 million singles and the only British act to have three number one singles in both the UK and the US. Their songs had been recorded in 12 languages and sold in 50 countries.

George Michael lies on a bed watching television in a
hotel room in Sydney, Australia during the 1985 world tour
in January 1985. 'The Big Tour'

Both George and Michael were determined to go out on a high and released a farewell single, The Edge of Heaven, which reached number one in June, plus a greatest hits album called The Final. They also performed a farewell concert, also called The Final on June 28, 1986 in front of 72,000 fans in Wembley Stadium. More than a million fans are said to have applied for tickets.

As well as being one of the hottest tickets around that year, when the day of the concert dawned it was also one of the hottest temperature wise. Special guests Elton John and Simon LeBon of old Wham! rivals Duran Duran further delighted the crowd.

When Andrew and George embraced after the final encore the screaming fans went wild. George later described the concert as having gone by in a blur, explaining that; 'It was such a big deal you know, and it was such a big thing to try and do at the time, you know, a stadium, to try and say goodbye. I wish that I could go through it again at the proper speed because it felt like it went past in an hour. And, I don't really remember much about it. I was so kind of... it was such a mixture of being sad that it was over, and excited that many people were there to see us, you know. So I kind of wish that I could go through that again'.

BUT WHEN IT WAS OVER - GEORGE HAD FREEDOM AT LAST........BUT IT WASN'T TO BE ALL THAT HE HAD HOPED.

41

George Michael lies on a bed watching television in a hotel room in Sydney, Australia during the 1985 world tour in January 1985. 'The Big Tour'

1986 - 1989

FREEDOM

Going solo, aged just 23, seemed an easy transition for George who was already a veteran performer, having achieved his teenage dream of becoming one of biggest and brightest pop stars in the world. He thought he knew who he was and what kind of music he wanted to make and hoped that he could 'uncreate' his Wham! persona and become more real.

His first solo number one (as Careless Whisper came out while he was still in Wham!) was A Different Corner in 1986 – a genuine attempt at being 'real' as he wrote it about a person who did not return his affections. A slow and sombre number, he performed it dressed in white and standing in a white room. He seemed to be saying that despite fame and fortune he was still a vulnerable human being.

George explained: 'It was the first time I used my own experience and emotions for a song. It was totally therapeutic, I completely exorcised that little part of my life. Careless Whisper never moved me like that.'

His solo career got off to a fantastic boost when early in 1987 he was involved in a one-off project with one of his favourite artists, the soul legend Aretha Franklin. Their duet I Knew You Were Waiting For Me, written by Dennis Morgan and Simon Climie, was a number one hit in the UK and the US, giving Aretha her only UK number one and first top 10 hit since I Say A Little Prayer in 1967. It was George's third consecutive number one after Careless Whisper and A Different Corner and helped him to become even more famous in America.

Then later that year came his magnum opus - the behemoth

that is his first solo album Faith. To date this has sold more than 25 million copies and was more successful than anything George had achieved with Wham. It was urban-pop at its best and a triumph for George who had written and produced every track himself, as well as playing several different instruments and contributing most of the vocals, including back up tracks.

Save the odd niggle (reviewer Mark Coleman did not rate Kissing a Fool) , Rolling Stone magazine described Faith as displaying George's 'intuitive understanding of pop music and his increasingly intelligent use of his power to communicate to an ever-growing audience'. Steve Huey from AllMusic said the album was 'a superbly crafted mainstream pop/rock masterpiece ...one of the finest pop albums of the 80s.'

Yet George did not feel Faith was a pop album, telling the American music magazine SPIN in 1987, that he believed the album was musically sophisticated, resembling the black pop and dance records he was listening to around that time.

Whatever the musical definition, George's fans loved it and Faith topped the album charts on both sides of the Atlantic. Four tracks from the album also made number one in the States - Faith, Father Figure, One More Try and Monkey - and it won Album of the Year at the Grammy Awards.

Another famous track from this album is I Want Your Sex, which was the first single release and gained even more publicity for the album by being banned from several radio stations. Including the lines, 'Sex is natural, sex is good, not everybody does it, but everybody should', it signalled that

George Michael, studio portrait, London, 1987

his boy band innocence was over. It also cemented George's heterosexual image when it was promoted with a video depicting him with his then real-life girlfriend and muse, American model Cathy Jeung. Sensual scenes included plenty of bare flesh and splashing water and George writing the words 'explore' and 'monogamy' on Cathy's leg.

George released a statement defending the song, which was actually an ode to monogamy. 'The emphasis of the AIDS campaign has been on safe sex, but the campaign has missed relationships. It's missed emotion. It's missed monogamy. 'I Want Your Sex' is about attaching lust to love, not just to strangers', he said.

Following the album's release, George set off on his first solo tour involving nine-months on the road performing 137 dates. While in Australia he suffered laryngitis and his voice got worse over the next few dates. A medical examination revealed a cyst on his on his vocal cords, requiring throat surgery.

It was a huge worry to him at the time; 'I genuinely thought, 'This is what happens. This is when you lose it',' he told The Big Issue in 1996. But luckily all went well with the operation and his career continued to flourish,

He was huge in the United States, where fame borders on deification, and he really couldn't deal with it. As the Rolling Stone's writer Greg Pond put it: 'He is only 24 – three years younger than Prince, five years younger than Michael Jackson, and outselling both of them. He is ridiculously famous; he has more money than he can spend. And for most of his brief career, he has had virtually no artistic credibility.'

By the time of his 25th birthday on 25 June 1988 George celebrated as a very successful solo performer. On the day itself he played the third of three dates at the NEC in Birmingham and was surprised on stage when Andrew appeared, along with his family, to present him with a giant birthday cake.

Wham! perform at their farewell concert, entitled 'The Final' at Wembley Stadium, 28th June 1986

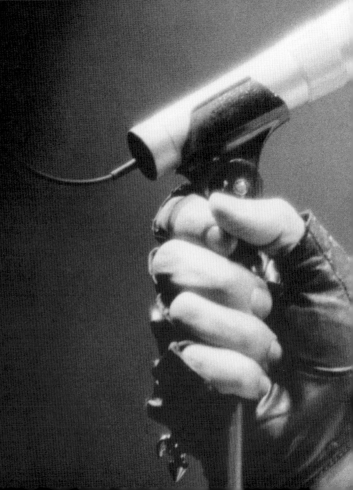

George Michael performing on stage during the
Japanese/Australasian leg of his Faith World Tour,
February-March 1988

Andrew led the audience in singing Happy Birthday, and then joined George to perform on old Wham! number one hit; 'I'm Your Man'.

And George undoubtedly was the man of the moment. He was at the top of his game by the time the tour ended in July 1989. The spotlight was on him, the cameras flashed, but overall George was growing increasingly uncomfortable with having his picture taken. There's a clue on the cover of Faith, where George's head is away from the camera, snuggled inside the lining of his leather jacket. The trouble was George had grown to be an extremely attractive man and his penchant for leather, stubble and flashes of gold in his earrings and hair only added to the attraction for his legion of female fans.

Despite this fame and the fact that outwardly he appeared cool, edgy, and sexy, George was actually floundering again, weighed down by the expectations up him, trapped again in an image which wasn't really who he was. 'George Michael turned the Orange Bowl into a steaming bubbling caldron of horniness on Saturday night', said The Miami Herald of his performance there.

Perhaps naively, he had not fully appreciated how the media interest in Andrew had taken the heat off him personally. Plus, by working with his close friend, he had always had emotional support and stability at close hand, both on and off stage. Without Andrew's back up, he felt very alone and became increasingly unhappy. Aged just 25 he won a Brit Award as best British solo artist, yet he wasn't at all sure about his next move.

'I felt cornered by my own ambition,' George said later in a 2009 interview with The Huffington Post. 'I didn't have the self-control to restrain my ego, but I knew it was leading me further and further towards an explosive end. I was becoming absolutely massively popular as a heterosexual male. It hadn't occurred to me, when I went solo, that I would get a whole new generation of 13-year-old girls as fans from Faith, but it happened. And in here' – he touched his chest – 'in here I was gay'.

IT WAS A PROBLEM THAT WAS INESCAPABLE – HOW LONG COULD HE LAST LIVING A LIE?

George Michael performing on stage during the Japanese/Australasian leg of his Faith World Tour, February-March 1988

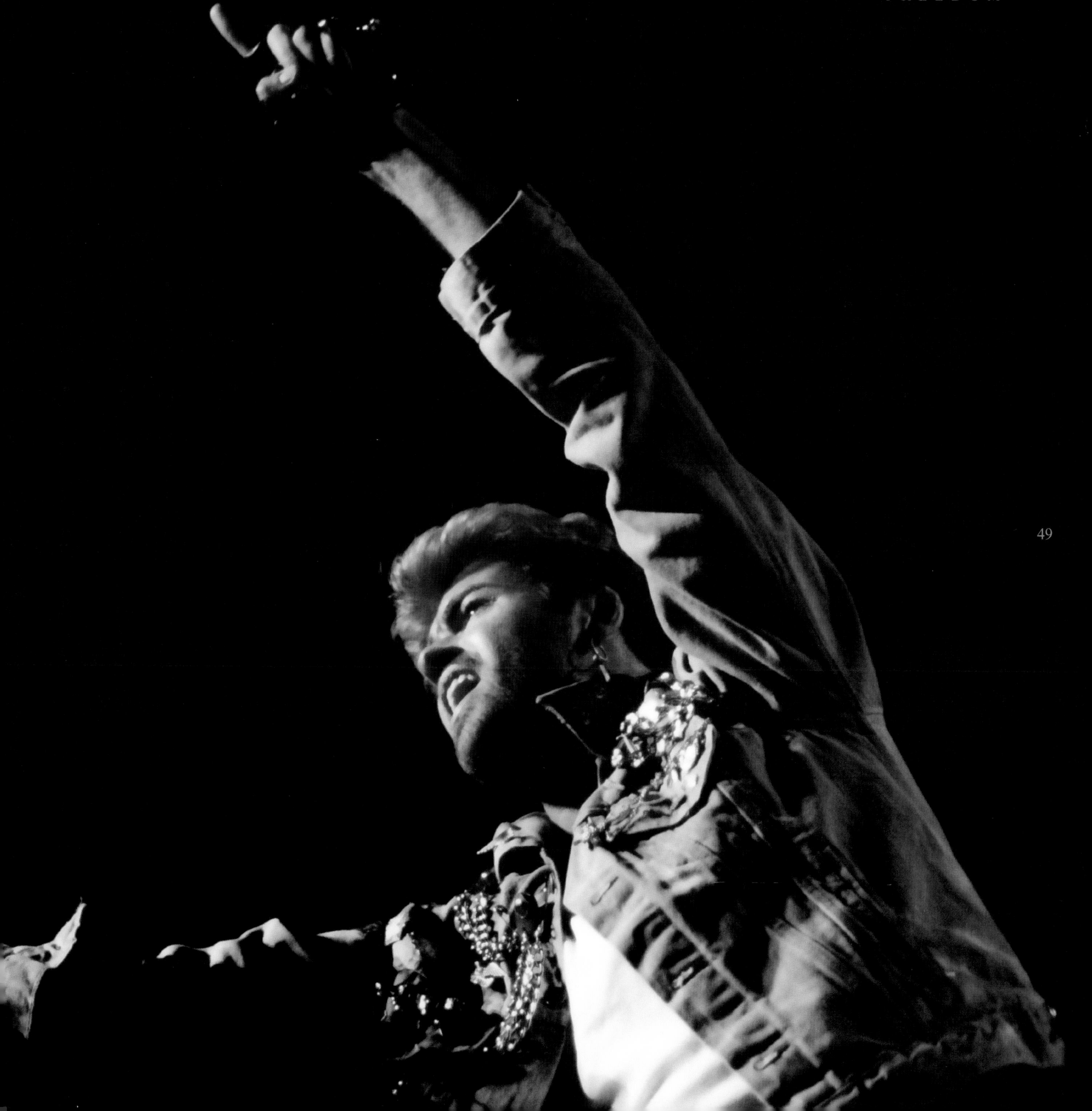

50

George Michael with girlfriend Kathy Yeung, on a train
looking at fans through the window, Japan, March 1988

51

52

LEFT: George Michael performing on stage during
the Japanese/Australasian leg of his Faith World Tour,
February-March 1988

ABOVE: George Michael performs on the Faith Tour, at
Ahoy, Rotterdam, Netherlands, 12th April 1988

54

George Michael on stage, Australia, March 1988

1 9 9 0 - 1 9 9 7
HEAL THE PAIN

George began the new decade still recovering from mental and physical exhaustion. Rumours about his sexual preferences were rife and he was heartily sick of the accompanying scrutiny.

So he returned to his roots, doing what he did best and what soothed his soul -which was to make music - and set to work on his second solo album, Listen Without Prejudice (Vol 1). But this time he was determined it would be released on his terms and he intended to take a back seat regarding promotion. The album cover shows part of a 1940s photograph 'Crowd at Coney Island' rather than an image of George.

The traditionally 'tricky' second album is usually surrounded by great expectation and this was certainly the case for George when following up on such a huge success as Faith.

Released on September 3, 1990, Listen Without Prejudice was a clear demonstration that George wanted to be taken more seriously as a musician and be true to himself, playing down his credentials as a heterosexual sex symbol. This is most striking in the track Freedom '90, an autobiographical take on his time in Wham! and seemingly describing his attempt to shift direction. George's lyrics even hinted at his sexual orientation, including the lines 'I think there's something you should know/ I think it's time I told you so ... there's someone else inside of me, someone else I've got to be.. All we have to do is take these lies and make them true'.

But George did not want to tour to promote the album, nor to make any videos. This latter problem was solved by employing a cast of super models to lip sync the song.

Linda Evangelista, Christy Turlington, Tatjana Patitz, Naomi Campbell and Cindy Crawford were among the most beautiful women in the world at that time. They lip synced a verse each, while during each of the three choruses a leather jacket, a guitar and a Wurlitzer jukebox – all symbols from Faith - were shown going up in flames.

George had had enough of fame and come to believe that the camera was his enemy. Aged just 27, he had already been world famous for almost 10 years and had had enough. After giving an interview to the Los Angeles Times' Calendar magazine complaining about fame – and refusing to have his picture taken to accompany the piece - he received a surprising rebuke from singing legend Frank Sinatra. Frank wrote an open-letter to George, published afterwards in the same magazine, warning George to be more appreciative of his lot in life. 'Come on George, loosen up......', Frank wrote. '......no more of that talk about 'the tragedy of fame'. The tragedy of fame is when no one shows up and you're singing to the cleaning lady in some empty joint that hasn't seen a paying customer since Saint Swithin's day.

'Those who have talent must hug it, embrace it, nurture it and share it lest it be taken away from you as fast as it was loaned to you. Trust me. I've been there,' counselled Frank.

But there was no dissuading George who took a hiatus from the whole showbiz shebang until 1996.

Listen Without Prejudice was of course a hit – selling more than eight million copies around the world – but nothing

56

like as huge as Faith. It was an entirely different album - an altogether quieter, more solemn collection of tracks, featuring a more acoustic sound, and did not garner quite the same ecstatic reviews. Rumours abounded that George had more dance music planned for release in 'Volume 2'.

The album did well in the UK, debuting at number one, spending 34 consecutive weeks in the top 20 and winning the 1991 Brit Award for Best British album.

There was a more muted reaction in the US where critics had their reservations. 'So no more breathless, pushy, addictive pop tunes like his '87 smash 'I Want Your Sex',' said Entertainment Weekly's review. 'If Listen Without Prejudice starts a trend among Michael's pop generation to move beyond image to integrity it could make 'rock and roll TV' sound more consistently and convincingly like music,' opined Rolling Stone. AllMusic agreed that George had 'turned inward, trying to gain critical acclaim as well as sales......[it is] not an entirely successful effort; Michael has cut back on the effortless hooks and melodies that crammed not only Faith, but also his singles with Wham! and his socially conscious lyrics tend to be heavy handed'.

George's refusal to appear in videos and tours to promote the album had consequences on sales, particularly in America where it was a commercial disappointment, and caused a massive rift between him and his record company Sony. Sales in the States amounted to barely two million, a poor showing compared to the seven million sales clocked up by Faith. Notwithstanding the fact he wanted a greatly reduced involvement in publicity, George took Sony to court in 1992, accusing the company of soft promotional support, amongst other legal infractions as he attempted to break free from his recording contract. Hence there was never to be a Listen Without Prejudice (Vol 2).

But before the case came to court something massive was

happening in George's personal life – he fell in love for the first time, at the age of 27.

It happened while George was performing in Brazil at the Rock in Rio concert in January 1991. The object of his affections, his first true love, was a fashion designer called Anselmo Feleppa. Accounts of their first meeting vary slightly, George once spoke of seeing him in the audience, but, on his Desert Island Discs interview, said that he first spotted him across a hotel lobby. Whichever way it happened there was evidently an instant attraction and Anselmo returned with George to LA. 'Anselmo broke down my Victorian restraint and really showed me how to live, how to relax, how to enjoy life,' George said. He later described the Brazilian designer as a 'saviour', who helped him come to terms with his sexuality.

'There have only been three times I've really fallen for anyone. And each time, on first sight, something has clicked that told me I was going to know that person. It happened with Anselmo across a lobby'.

Up until that time of monogamy with Anselmo, George had had many sexual experiences, gay and straight. In fact his sexual appetite would get him into trouble throughout his life. But he always practised safe sex, which protected him from AIDS and HIV, whereas Anselmo had not been so fortunate. After taking a medical test early on in their relationship, Anselmo discovered that he was HIV positive – a death sentence at that time before effective therapies became available. They had been together just six months before Anselmo's diagnosis.

George described Christmas 1991 as 'the darkest, most frightening time in my life' as he and his secret love awaited the results of AIDS tests. George visited his family in the UK, while Anselmo was in LA. 'I sat at the Christmas table not knowing whether my partner, who the people around the

58

table did not know about ... not knowing whether the man I was in love with was terminally ill, therefore not knowing whether I was, potentially, terminally ill,' he said subsequently. 'I remember looking at the sky and saying, 'Don't you dare do this to me!'

Unfortunately there was bad news – the result was positive and Anselmo had the HIV virus and was terminally ill. George was distraught but had to keep everything he was going through a secret because still no-one in his wider family, nor his fan base, knew that he was gay.

'In 1991 it was terrifying news', George said in an interview with the Independent newspaper. 'I couldn't go through it with my family because I didn't know how to share it with them; they didn't know I was gay. I couldn't tell my closest friends because Anselmo didn't want me to.... the isolation was just crazy.'

Although George had long since made up with his father, after vindicating his decision to go into music, he still hadn't felt ready to share the details of his love life. Also George knew that it would hit his mother hard. Her brother Colin had taken his own life the day after George was born. George understood that one of the reasons for his depression was his homosexuality – difficult to discuss in those days. So he didn't want to upset his mother by raking this up and making her fear her son might suffer similarly one day. Colin's story stayed with George throughout his life and he referenced it through the song, My Mother had a Brother on the Patience album;

So George kept his secret and went through the motions as Anselmo's disease progressed.

Another especially tough time came in the midst of Anselmo's illness in April 1992 when George took part in the Freddie Mercury Tribute concert. Freddie – another of George's childhood heroes with whom he'd become friendly - had died of an AIDS-related complication just six months earlier and the memorial concert was to raise funds for AIDS research. As George performed no one around him had any idea of his personal connection to the illness as he faced his own lover's mortality.

'I went out there knowing I had to honour Freddie Mercury and I had to pray for Anselmo,' George recalled in the documentary Freedom.

'I just wanted to die inside. I was so overwhelmed by singing the songs of this man I had worshipped as a child, who had passed away in the same manner my first living partner was going to experience.

'The performance most well-known in my career was sung to my lover who was dying.'

The end came when Anselmo was back visiting family in Brazil, without George. He died of an AIDS-related complication, a brain haemorrhage, in March 1993.

George was devastated. The one positive to come out of the tragedy was that George wrote a letter to his parents the day after losing Anselmo to tell them what had happened and that he was gay. Both his parents took it well. Lesley was understandably sad that George had struggled with the realisation by himself for so long and wanted to do all she could in the future to support him. Jack was similarly keen to let George know he was ok with it – in contrast to the disapproval he voiced at his son's original career choice.

'I genuinely feel that although his son is gay and not going to

59

Andrew Ridgeley appearing with George Michael at a solo performance at Rock In Rio III, 1991

60

61

Elton John on stage with George Michael performing live
in the early 1990's

give him any grand kids, my dad's consolation is that I have done well in life,' George told GQ in a later interview. 'It's sad, but I do feel success can negate a parent's disappointment'.

Looking back on the relationship and loss, which he says he never got over, George later said; 'I think he went to Brazil because he feared what my fame would do to him and his family if he got treatment elsewhere. I was devastated by that.

'It was tragic that I lost him, but it was a wonderful experience meeting him.'

Anselmo's death marked the start of a very dark period in George's life as he struggled to get over the loss of his lover. Drugs and depression were to take him over. His manager at that time, Simon Napier-Bell said; 'One saw George go through a terrible down period. You could see that he was withdrawn, there were rumours from everybody that he was doing a lot of drugs, and when he did do an interview, he would be openly smoking nonstop joints.'

But alongside the grief George also felt anger that Anselmo had been taken from him. He subsequently came to believe that it was this raging at the unfairness of his situation that fuelled him to pursue the court case with Sony. Proceedings came to a head in court in 1993.

Panayiotou and others v Sony Music Entertainment (UK) Ltd was a landmark case for the recording industry because of the precedent it could have set regarding long-term contracts in the music industry generally.

As well as alleging that Sony under-promoted his new album, George claimed that the contract stopped him from changing record label and managing his professional image as he saw fit. George famously described this 'imbalanced' relationship between label and artist as being akin to 'professional slavery'.

But in his ruling on June 1, 1994, Justice Jonathan Parker wholly rejected George's claims and judged that the Sony contracts were 'fair and reasonable.'

Speaking at a news conference after the verdict George said it meant that ...'In fact there is no such thing as resignation for an artist in the music industry. Effectively, you sign a piece of paper at the beginning of your career and you are expected to live with that decision, good or bad, for the rest of your professional life'.

Refusing to record for Sony and unable to move to another label, George's music-making was effectively on hold for the next five years. Speaking on the Freedom documentary he later produced, his friend and former manager David Austin confirmed that the case also killed George's career in the USA, 'He was a guy who was firing on all four cylinders and it just, it blew that candle out in the US without a doubt.'

Losing the case prevented him from releasing any new material for two years and obliged him to pay Sony $30m -$40m (£24m-£33m) to release him.

George effectively went into seclusion. He was a man of principle – that's what the case was about for him. He freely admitted he didn't really need any more money and just wanted to make points about creative control, musical direction and mutual respect between artist and label, contesting that it was 'ridiculous' to be held to a contract you had signed as a young and vulnerable artist aged 18, for an entire professional career.

Eventually David Geffen's start-up label Dreamworks SKG and Virgin bought out his Sony contract, allowing George to start work again. The result was the 1996 release of the bittersweet album, Older, and its opening track, the mournful and haunting seven-minute-long Jesus to a Child – a tribute

George Michael performs on stage at the Freddie Mercury Tribute Concert for AIDS Awareness at Wembley Stadium, April 20th 1992

63

to Anselmo - released as a single in 1996 and one of his most personal works.

'I never want to be so inspired again by plummeting such depths of emotion', he later said. Having sunk into a major depression after losing Anselmo and beginning to smoke the daily spliffs of cannabis which became a big part of his life and downfall, it was only to be expected that he would produce such a melancholic piece of work.

Reviews for Older were generally favourable, though as with Listen without Prejudice, it went down better in the UK than the US.

Because the press and public didn't know what had been going on with him personally, the album seemed to lack context.

'Although he occasionally sounds like the Prozac queen Elizabeth Wurtzel singing 'It's My Party' in an empty karaoke bar, for those who can get past Michael's pretentious melancholy, Older is a surprisingly enjoyable record,' said Rolling Stone - unaware that the melancholy was in fact genuine.

'Michael hasn't lost his talent for writing pop songs as contagious as the Ebola virus, if only slightly more cheery', the Rolling Stone review continued.

Agreeing it was a gloomy collection of tracks, AllMusic said it made 'Listen Without Prejudice sound like Faith...'Although Michael's skills as a pop craftsman still shine through, his earnestness sinks the album. It is one thing to be mature and another to be boring.'

And a mystified Entertainment Weekly unwittingly got it spot on when they wrote,' Something happened to Michael at the

dawn of the decade, and whatever it is, he can't shake it off.'

But George's loyal fans were delighted to have some new material from their idol - 'Thank you for waiting,' he had written on the back of the Older album, acknowledging the gap in his output. This time he was back on the cover - albeit half in shadow - looking altogether different with a moustache, goatee beard and closely cropped hair. More clues as to his sexuality?

Speaking to Oprah Winfrey George said later, 'The way my image changed in Europe was that I looked very different, I had very short hair—I had really a kind of gay look in a way. I think I was trying to tell people I was okay with it [being gay], I just really didn't want to share it with journalists..... Older was a tribute to Anselmo, really; there was a dedication to him on the album and fairly obvious male references. To my fans and the people that were really listening, I felt like I was trying to come out with them.'

The album sold well - 1.8 million copies in the UK alone - and produced a record-breaking six top three hit singles in two years.

That same year he was voted Best British Male at the Brits and the MTV Europe awards, as well as picking up another Ivor Novello award as Songwriter of The Year.

He also performed his first concert in years, featuring in the MTV Unplugged series. 'I just lost myself in singing that night,' he said later. 'I am so glad my mum was there and I'm so glad for the first time ever, the only time ever on film, I actually said hello to my mum in the audience. It was the last time she saw me play.'

For George was to suffer another huge blow that year when his beloved mother Lesley was diagnosed with terminal skin

George Michael performs on stage at the Freddie Mercury Tribute Concert for AIDS Awareness at Wembley Stadium, April 20th 1992

cancer. She died in February 1997, less than a year after her diagnosis, after one last Christmas with her family.

George took it hard – his second massive loss in five years. 'I was so spiritually crushed after my mum died. So crushed and felt so bloody picked on by the gods. For all of my adult life she was phenomenal. Terrible, horrible loss,' George said. 'I'd never felt that kind of depression. It was something different to grief. It was on top of grief, I was grieving for my mother still, but it was something else. It was the darkest time.'

A saving grace was that having emerged from his self-imposed exile George had found some personal happiness with a new lover, Kenny Goss, a charming Texan entrepreneur. He credits Kenny with having helped him through the terrible depression he experienced after the death of his mother. But nevertheless losing Lesley was almost too much to bear and his use of strong cannabis and Prozac increased.

Depression was an illness that ran in his family – as well has his Uncle Colin, his maternal grandfather had also suffered and eventually committed suicide.

The 1990s overall were dark days of drugs, depression and loss for George who credited Kenny Goss with helping him through it all.

'If he hadn't been around, I think my life would have been in danger, in terms of me,' George said. 'After Mum's death in 1997, when I couldn't write and I felt really worthless, I don't think I could have taken it really. I think I might have been one of those cowards who choose a nasty way out.

'.... [Kenny] was there to put his arms around me and remind me there was something positive going on.'

The loss of Anselmo and his mother within a handful of years shocked George to his core and left him very fearful about how further such events might floor him. He spoke in an interview with GQ magazine about the worry of losing Kenny who he described as an 'angel, sent to me at exactly the right moment'.

He went on to describe that his biggest problem at that time was fear of loss. 'I fear Kenny's death far more than my own', he said in an interview with GQ magazine. 'I don't want to outlive him. I'd rather have a short life and not have to go through being torn apart again. Kenny has to travel a lot with his job and we have fights before he flies because I try and get him to avoid British Airways or American Airlines in case he falls victim to a terrorist attack. When he leaves me, I panic. I can't relax until he's called to say he's arrived safely. But when I fly, I don't care and get straight on BA.'

His run of bad luck continued, including a serious back operation and the death of his beloved dog Hippy the Labrador. He had attempted to prepare for the loss of Hippy by buying a puppy beforehand, but his plans were thwarted in a horrible way when the puppy drowned in the Thames.

It did appear that fortune did not favour him for a while.

But then something happened which could have been another huge blow, but actually turned out to be almost a blessing in disguise.

HE WAS OUTED AND OVERNIGHT THE WORLD KNEW FOR SURE THAT HE WAS GAY.

George Michael at the MTV awards, 1995

68

Lisa Stansfield and George Michael performing
at the Freddie Mercury Tribute Concert for AIDS
Awareness, at Wembley Stadium, London, 20 April 1992

O U T S I D E

George had an open relationship with Kenny Goss - on his side at least - and was famously into anonymous sex. So he continued his habitual cruising and pursued his predilection for anonymous sex with strangers.

However one April afternoon he struck unlucky when he was arrested in a Los Angeles public toilet in the Will Rogers Memorial Park by Beverly Hills police for 'engaging in a lewd act'. George maintained the whole thing was a set up - the arresting officer, Marcelo Rodriguez had been in plain clothes, working under cover.

But in fact it left him better off. At last his secret was out and a burden was lifted.

'I knew at some time I was going to get outed' George said. 'It took me a year to admit that it was subconsciously deliberate'.

His reaction to the whole debacle was to style it out. Rather than hide away in shame, he endeared himself to the public by reacting with humour. The very next day, with the press crowded around his house, he went out to a local restaurant. In interviews afterwards he would often joke about it.

He also used the arrest as inspiration for more music. His hit single Outside was accompanied by a video parodying the whole affair and showing that he was not ashamed. It included depictions of gay and heterosexual couples having sex 'in the sunshine' and in public toilets and featured a disco-dancing George dressed as a police officer. The undercover

police officer who had arrested George filed a $10 million lawsuit claiming that the video caused him mental and emotional distress, but the claim was dismissed.

The song was a huge hit for George, reaching number two in the UK charts and was included on his solo hits collection titled Ladies & Gentlemen: The Best of George Michael released on November 9 that year. Again his largely female fans forgave him. Speaking with CNN that year George discussed the matter of having been a pin up for women and clarified that he hadn't deliberately set out to deceive. 'I do want people to know that the songs I wrote when I was with women were really about women, and the songs I've written since have been, fairly obviously, about men.... I want people to know, especially people who love the earlier stuff, if they were young girls at the time, whatever, there was no bullsh*t there.'

He was also sorry if the gay community had felt upset about his years of - if not denial exactly, then of being coy about his true sexuality. 'By the time I'd kind of worked out what it was, and I'd stopped having relationships with women, I was just so indignant about the way I had been treated until then, I just thought, well, I'll just hold on to this. They [the media] don't need to know'.

Instead of ruining his career the 'accidental' public 'outing' set him free from press speculation and inner turmoil. Kenny, who forgave the indiscretion, was now able to be officially acknowledged as George's partner.

But it wasn't all rosy - in America where attitudes can be more puritanical, the incident didn't play so well and his career there took another hit. The incident in the Will Rogers

George Michael performing at a benefit concert for the NetAid anti-poverty charity, Wembley Stadium, London, 15th June 1999

74

Park was the beginning of the end of his career in America, changing the country and the singer's views of each other. George was to sell his home in Beverly Hills and only visited the country now and again for the rest of his life.

Things weren't helped when his 1999 album Songs from the Last Century failed to make a good impression – the feeling being that his covers were nowhere as good as the iconic originals. Not doubting that George genuinely admired the numbers he chose, Stephen Thomas Erlewinen from AllMusic captured the feeling of many when he wrote ' Certainly, Songs from the Last Century isn't a major work; it's a way for Michael to decompress and have some fun, and the diehards who stuck with him through the turbulent '90s are likely to be charmed.'

It became George's only solo album to miss out on the number one spot Rather less kindly, NME said 'Outside, plus video, was funny and vital, so it's strange that he [George] should decide to sleepwalk out of the '90s dressed in borrowed pyjamas'.

He may not have been sleepwalking as much as enjoying being in a stable place and recovering from all the drama and death he'd experienced.

In an interview with the Independent newspaper he explained that his recovery started around this time after '....12 years of depression and fear, and lots of other s**t. I swear to God it was like I had a curse on me. I couldn't believe how much God was piling on at once. There was so much death around me, I can't tell you'.

He spent most of his time at his 16th Century home in Goring-on Thames in Oxfordshire, about an hour from London; 'my dear, beautiful house' as he called it. With Kenny and his two new dogs, Meg and Abby, it was a picture of domestic bliss – for a time.

BUT IT WASN'T LONG BEFORE GEORGE WAS INVOLVED IN ANOTHER CONTROVERSY.

George Michael performing at a benefit concert for the NetAid anti-poverty charity, Wembley Stadium, London, 15th June 1999

GETTING OVER HIS FREEEK OUT

Having been largely out of the public eye for a few years, George regained some creative oomph and reappeared in 2002 with a thumping dance track Freeek, taken from his forthcoming album 'Patience'.

Freeek was accompanied by a hugely expensive sci-fi style video, directed by leading music video producer Joseph Kahn, packed with raunchy scenes including rubber, leashes and cyborgs.

'When I thought of the song, I wanted it to represent the victory of commerce and certain types of commerce around sex over all of us,' George explained. 'In other words, there's so much money involved, I wanted Freeek to sound like this kind of steamroller of sex that you couldn't get out of its way.'

It was a big hit in the UK and around Europe.

The next single from the still unreleased Patience caused massive controversy and saw George pilloried for daring to enter the arena of politics.
Shoot The Dog was hugely critical of the foreign policy being pursued by UK Prime Minister Tony Blair and US president George W Bush in the run up to the Iraq war.

The song was accompanied by a political satirical cartoon video depicting Blair as Bush's poodle- 'Good Puppy' - and included controversial images of Cherie Blair, The Queen and Prince Charles. 'If it stimulates debate and makes people dance and laugh I think it will have done it's job' said George.

But it made him a hate figure and the target of homophobic abuse from some quarters of the press and music industry.

Fellow pop star Noel Gallagher of Oasis appeared to challenge George's right to an opinion, saying; 'This is the guy who hid who he actually was from the public for 20 years, and now all of a sudden he's got something to say about the way of the world. I find it ***ing laughable!'.

The press was also turning on him, accusing him of being anti-American and insensitive in the wake of the September 11 terror attacks the previous year.

'I just thought, it's so illogical that because somebody is closeted they wouldn't have the right to talk about the potential of a war,' George said of the furore.

'[But] ..it was so stupid not to expect what I got, not just on a political level but on the level of .... listen these people don't like you; they find it hard enough taking it coming from a pop star let alone one they think is too snotty to talk to them in general. I knew that a lot of these papers that were centre left and actually agreed with me, but they were still jumping up and down on me. So I did start to take that personally.'

The Sun newspaper in London ran a front page mocking the fact that the song wasn't to be released in America. Headlined

'Coward', the article accused George of being 'scared to release it in the States in case it offends those fans he still has left. What a cop-out'.

Eventually George issued a statement, explaining his motives and hoping to set the record straight:

'The song and video in question is definitely not an attempt to express anti-American sentiment, nor an attempt to condone the actions of Al-Qaeda.

'I have lived with an American citizen for the past six years and have had a home there for the past 10. And I would never knowingly disrespect the feelings of a nation, which has suffered so much loss, so recently, for any reason'.

'Shoot the Dog is simply my attempt to contribute to the public debate that I feel should be taking place regarding Iraq and Saddam Hussein'.

'I have tried to convey my message with humour, because the public is rightfully scared of these issues, and humour has often been a useful aide to political debate'.

'And believe me, however irreverent I may be of Mr Blair and Mr Bush, my intentions are genuinely to do something, however small, to protect all of us, the people I love, and the people you love, from a disaster that we have the power to avoid'.
'The record was never intended for American release for the precise reason that I felt it could be misread in this very way and it makes me truly sad that this press statement has been necessary'.

It was signed, 'Sincerely, George Michael'.

Eventually, Patience was released in March 2004– a full eight years since his last studio album - and went straight to the top of the charts.

While it was not surprising that it was a hit, it was mystifying to many that George released it through his old adversary Sony who said;' We are delighted to be working again with one of the greatest recording artists this country had ever produced, who has made another classic album'.

They simply offered the best deal.

The record label had never bad-mouthed George, even at the height of the court proceedings, and they did still own most of his back catalogue.

Patience was a sophisticated mix of ballads and disco tracks and spawned six hit singles in total, including Flawless and Amazing. Flawless was a tribute to Kenny Goss and gave George what was to be his last top 10 single in the US.

'Amazing reminds me of Wham! more than anything else I've done,' he once said. 'The work I've done over the last 12 years might have a certain intensity or depth, but nothing has had the energy of the earlier work. I think it's come with the relief of feeling good again.'

However two of the tracks were more downbeat, Cars and Trains and My Mother Had a Brother both handling the subject of suicide.

George said that Patience would be the last album to go on sale to the public as a physical release. He said that in future he would want to make his music available for fans to download in return for a donation to charity. He hoped that such a move would take the pressure off him and allow him more of a private life.

Creatively revived, George felt able to return to the stage. He appeared with Paul McCartney during his set for Live 8 in 2005 where the pair sang 'Drive my Car'.

He also set about planning a world tour 25 LIVE, also known as the 25th Anniversary Tour for 2006/7.

He'd been away for 15 years – but the fans were waiting with open arms to welcome him back. George was knocked out by their loyalty and warmth. The 25 Live tour was billed as a 'celebration of his 25-year-career in music' and was a smash hit, a commercial and creative triumph – grossing over $2m. A Greatest Hits album followed at the end of 2006 and the tour was extended into 2007 due to demand.

During the tour George was booked to perform as the first pop act at the newly reopened Wembley Stadium, but he only just made it when his scheduled appearance was nearly de-railed by more drama.

There was still speculation about his sex life and use of drugs. He had a well- documented penchant for cannabis and liquid ecstasy and was arrested on suspicion of possessing class C drugs after being found slumped at the wheel of a car in London in February 2006.

Worse was to come when, on October 1, 2006 after returning from a concert in Paris, George was found semi-conscious at the wheel of his Mercedes in Cricklewood, north London. His defence lawyers claimed he was affected by tiredness and prescribed drugs including GHB and cannabis. He said he had been given a DVD of his most recent concert and had attempted to drive to another home he owned in north London to watch it as his machine was broken.

Witnesses said they had seen his car weaving into the wrong side of the road at around five to ten miles an hour in the early hours of the morning.

He had then stopped at traffic lights and remained stationary through several changes of the lights before pulling off in a way they thought might cause an accident.

The witnesses described his behaviour as being 'bewildered, frightened, confused' and apparently under the influence, as they described it, of drugs', when they approached the car.

The case came to court in June 2007 and George arrived at court smiling amid a scrum of press. Watching fans shouted, 'We love you George!' as he moved between car and courtroom. He looked well, dressed in black and with his customary sunglasses. He told the court he was 'ashamed' of his behaviour and admitted the charge of driving while unfit through drugs.

He was banned from driving for two years and ordered to undertake 100 hours community service. He was fortunate to escape a jail term as the very next day he was booked to play at the refurbished 90,000 seat Wembley Stadium – the first act to play there following its redevelopment.

The concert went ahead on June 9 and an apparently happy George played a two and a half hour set including songs from Wham! days as well as his solo career. He told the 90,000-strong crowd; 'I'm actually here, I don't believe it. For the most amazing, God-given 25 years, I thank you all.'

The Wembley venue was special to George as he had played it most memorably during Live Aid in 1985 and again for the Wham! farewell concert in 1986 and he was genuinely honoured to reopen the venue.

George Michael performs on stage for the finale at 'Live 8 London' in Hyde Park on July 2, 2005 in London, England

He also really appreciated that his success had continued as his audience grew older with him and accepted and enjoyed his music as it matured and explored more personal themes. His sexuality didn't seem to make a difference to his legion of female fans. Although marrying George was clearly no longer an option, women still held him in enormous affection and felt protective of him. His later brushes with the law and problems with drugs only served to make him more vulnerable.

But although always appreciative of his loyal fanbase, he was also often mystified, as he explained when he appeared on Desert Island Discs in 2007.

'You can't imagine what it is like playing to people who have been loyal to you for 25 years, who haven't seen you for 15. It's the most life-affirming thing I could have done. ...... I'm so grateful to them.'

'In a strange way I have spent much of the last 15, 20 years trying to derail my career because it never seems to suffer ...I suffer like crazy... but my career seems to right itself like a plastic duck in a bath. And I think in some ways I resent that'.

'Because you are rich and famous does not mean your life is problem-free. Problems are not greater or less than when I was 17, just different.

'I think I finally realised that one of the reasons my life has been so extreme and in some ways self-destructive, is that, it sounds arrogant, but I never had any feeling that my talent was going to let me down. I had a feeling that I had an advantage over a lot of other people in the industry, and a lot of people in my own life.'

At that time, he seemed to be in a good place, having found some peace and contentment in his life with Kenny. When pressed as to what was different, he said;' Well in all honesty nobody's died on me in years. It took me years to believe that these blows weren't going to keep coming.'

He also spoke about his relationship with marihuana and said he didn't think it was a big problem, nor getting in the way of

George Michael performs at Datch Forum on October 07, 2006 in Milan, Italy

On stage during his European tour, 'Symphonica' at the O2
Arena in Berlin on September 5, 2011

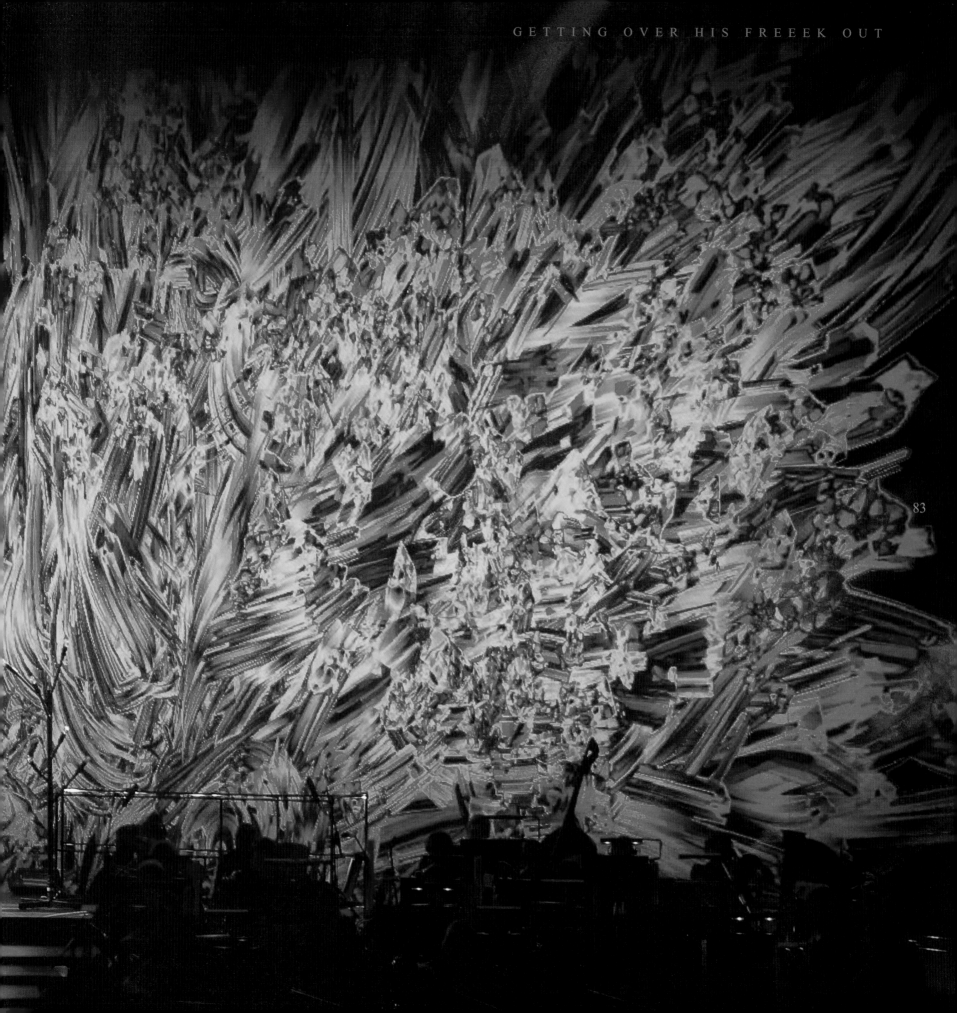

84

George Michael performs on stage in Bratislava, 25 May
2007 during his concert as part of his European Tour

George Michael performs during a concert in Amsterdam,
26 June 2007

his life in any way; 'I'm a happy man and I can afford it.'

The following year, in March 2008, a third extension of the 25 LIVE Tour was announced for North America – this was his first tour there for 17 years.

The tour eventually wound up with a series of 'Final' concerts – their name a nod to the final Wham! gig. There were two concerts at Earls Court in London named 'The Final Two, then 'The Final One' was played in in Copenhagen, Denmark, on 30 August 2009. But even after that dates were added in Australia, involving stops in Perth, Sydney, and later Melbourne in February/March 2010.

It seemed that George could have kept going for years such was the public appetite to see him perform. Perhaps it would have been better if he had. For on returning to London his problems with drugs reared their head again in another infamous brush with the law.

He'd been arrested during a break from touring in 2008, again in a public toilet, but this time on Hampstead Heath - an area he frequently cruised. This time he was cautioned by police for possession of a controlled substance.

At the time George said: 'I want to apologise to my fans for screwing up again, and to promise them I'll sort myself out. And to say sorry to everybody else, just for boring them.'

But he didn't manage to sort himself out. His relationship with Kenny Goss came to an end in 2009 - he had lost an emotional support once again. Kenny later said that there was no big bust up; 'Things just petered out.... There was no big event, no anger or hostility'.

But after that things appeared to go from bad to worse for George personally . He made another rather spectacular journey into the headlines after he was arrested after smashing his Range Rover into the front of a branch of Snappy Snaps near his home in Hampstead, north London on July 4, 2010.

This time he lost his licence for five years and received an eight-week prison sentence, of which he served four weeks.

Ever gentlemanly in his dealings with people, George apologised to the shop's manager, saying, 'I'm genuinely and sincerely sorry for smashing into your shop.'

His friends were worried for him – but he was hard to help, sometimes even publicly scoffing at any mention of the fact he might be struggling. He entered a period of self-imposed semi-retirement. If pressed he told people that he enjoyed a quiet life, walked his dogs and watched Coronation Street.

But by 2011 he seemed to be in a better place, with a renewed focus on his career. He was looking fitter, having lost weight after giving up the steroids he had previously taken to protect his voice.

He recorded a cover version of the Stevie Wonder song You and I (We Can Conquer The World) as a wedding gift for Prince William when he married Kate Middleton in April 2011 – the proceeds going to charity. George had been good friends with William's mother Diana, Princess of Wales. Sadly he was able to empathise with the Royal Princes William and his brother Harry following Diana's death, having felt the loss of his own mother Lesley so keenly.

Then he took to the road again with his Symphonic tour – an orchestral pop show, which began in 2011.

Symphonica was different from his previous shows in terms of arrangements and visuals. Technology had come on massively since his days with Wham! in the 1980s and George was keen to make the most of it. The tour was highly praised. His voice was in fine form, despite his ongoing enthusiasm for smoking.

Speaking about Symphonica he said: 'I like to challenge myself – to improve as a vocalist. And believe me, singing with an orchestra is one way to do it.'

In an interview with Morten Resen to promote the tour in Denmark, George discussed the ongoing pressures of fame saying that he coped 'as badly as ever ... I try very hard to thank my lucky stars and keep it in perspective and proportion, but it can be very tiring having a smiley face all day'.

The tour was briefly interrupted 45 dates in, when George came down with pneumonia which almost proved fatal. He was taken to hospital in Vienna and things were touch and go for a while. At the time the seriousness of his illness was played down, but afterwards a weak and tearful George told the press that his illness had been 'life-threatening' and explaining that the Austrian doctors had had to perform a tracheotomy during 'undoubtedly the worst time of my life'

'I'm incredibly, incredibly fortunate to be here and incredibly fortunate to have picked up this bug where I did, because apparently the hospital in Austria that they rushed me to was absolutely the best place in the world I could have been, to deal with pneumonia,' he told journalists. 'So I have to believe

George Michael attends a press conference to announce details of a new tour at The Royal Opera House on May 11, 2011 in London, England

In concert at the Verona Arena. Verona, Italy. 14th
September 2011

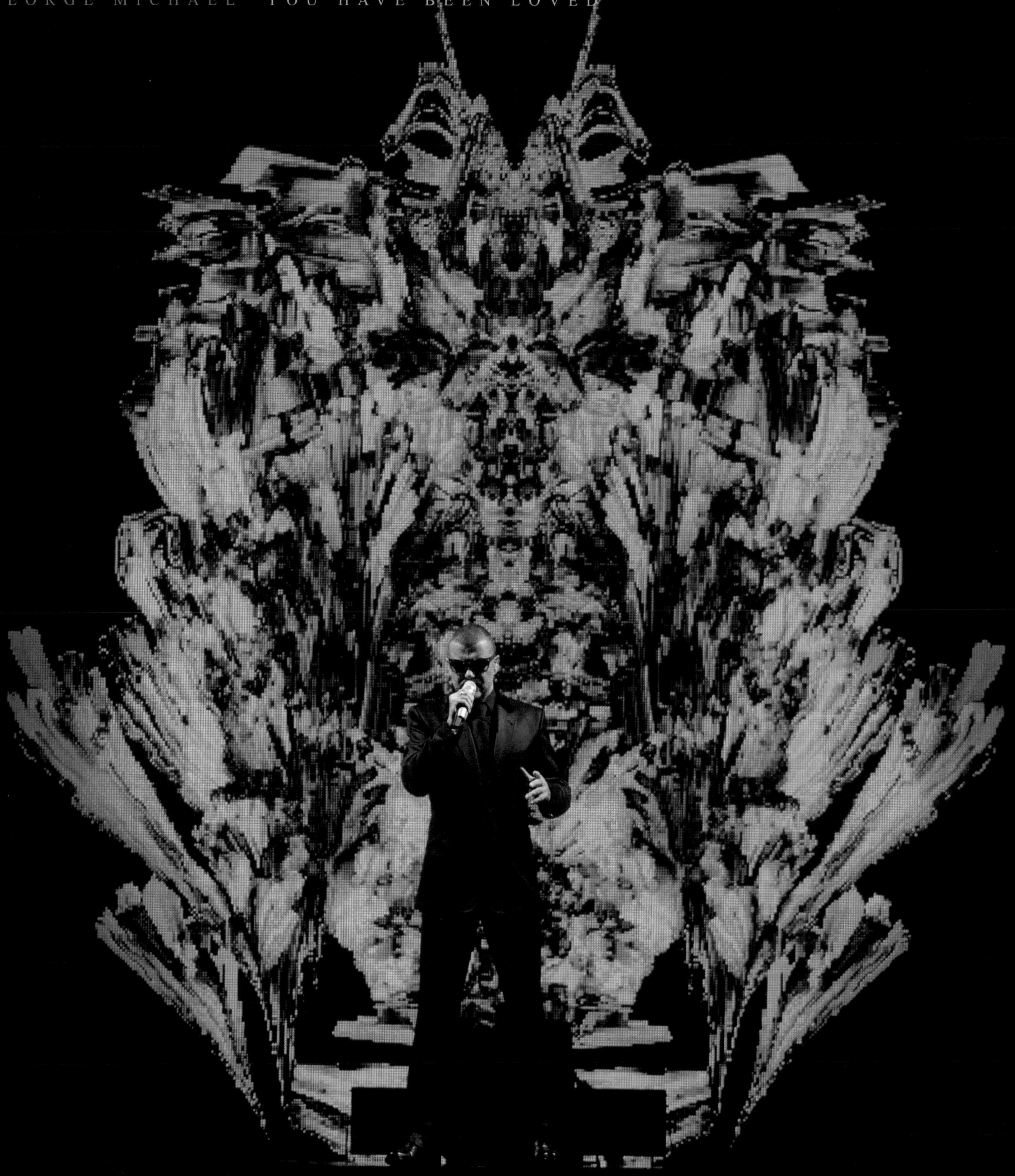

that somebody thinks I've still got some work to do here.

'I have an amazing, amazing life, and if I wasn't spiritual enough before the last four, five weeks then I certainly am now.'

Vowing to complete the tour, George added that he wanted to play one extra show for the doctors at AKH hospital in Vienna who had saved his life. He also performed at the closing ceremony of the London Olympics on August 12, 2012 where he sang Freedom 90 and a new song White Light, referencing his near-death experience

Yet, despite his initial elation at having survived a brush with death, the episode apparently sparked a major bout of anxiety and depression in George.

He found himself back in hospital with a bad head injury just 18 months later following a bizarre incident when he fell out of his chauffeur-driven car as it sped down the M1, close to the M25 in Hertfordshire. His publicist explained that George had been trying to adjust his door which was not properly closed, although there were rumours at the time that he had jumped out deliberately.

He was clearly troubled and in the grip of a bout of the horrible depression which had plagued him for the past 20 years.

He tried rehab and to wean himself of his antidepressants, there were reports of ambulances at his home, and rumours that he had moved on to harder drugs.

Yet through all his difficulties he continued to work – hoping that music might help him emerge from the fug. As he had said previously, his talent didn't usually let him down.

He worked to finish the Symphonica album, containing mostly live versions of songs from the 2011/12 world tour, which had been delayed by the death of its first producer Phil Ramone. It was released in March 2014

BUT WAS TO BE HIS SIXTH AND AS IT TURNED OUT FINAL RECORDING.

93

The Closing Ceremony on Day 16 of the London 2012
Olympic Games at Olympic Stadium on August 12, 2012

2016
LAST CHRISTMAS

Wham!'s seasonal hit Last Christmas was enjoying its annual bonanza on the airwaves when the news reports came through on Christmas Day 2016 that George had died suddenly, aged 53.

It ruined the day for his millions of fans, many of whom began trooping, in tears, to lay flowers at the front door of his home, Mill Cottage in Oxfordshire.

He was found dead in bed by his then boyfriend, hairdresser Fadi Fawaz who had come to collect him to go out for lunch. Reports said he had died from suspected heart failure, but toxicology tests would take place.

Tributes came from around the world, from those dear to him and from others just appreciative of his music.

Andrew Ridgeley said simply, on Twitter, 'Heartbroken at the loss of my beloved friend Yog'.

During a concert at Caesar's Palace in Las Vegas three days after George had died, a clearly emotional Elton John dedicated Don't Let The Sun Go Down On Me, to George, saying; ' ....apart from the music, which is outstanding, and for those of you who don't know his music go and listen to it. It stands up so brilliantly. What a singer. What a songwriter. But more than anything, as a human being, he was one of the kindest, sweetest, most generous people I've ever met. He gave so much money to so many great causes without telling anybody. He was constantly trying to help people. And the saddest thing is he

couldn't help himself. So I'm going to dedicate this song...and I just wish he was here to sing it with me.'

Paul McCartney said; 'George Michael's sweet soul music will live on even after his sudden death. Having worked with him on a number of occasions his great talent always shone through and his self-deprecating sense of humour made the experience even more pleasurable.'

Eventually, toxicology tests were concluded and the senior coroner for Oxfordshire issued a statement saying; 'As there is a confirmed natural cause of death, being dilated cardiomyopathy with myocarditis and fatty liver, the investigation is being discontinued and there is no need for an inquest or any further inquiries. No further updates will be provided and the family requests the media and public respect their privacy.'

Following the coroner's statement, George could be buried at last, and his funeral took place on March 29 2017. It was a low-key service in the tiny, 30-seat chapel at Highgate West Cemetery, attended by family including his 80-year old father Jack, and sisters Melanie and Yioda and close friends such as Andrew Ridgeley, Shirlie Holliman and Helen 'Pepsi DeMacque. Former boyfriend Kenny Goss was also there and said afterwards, 'I didn't cry. I just thought, 'That's him in there'.

'I pictured him being younger — aged 33 in an amazing suit with his Cartier watch on. I touched the coffin. It was reassuring to know he was resting in peace.'

Following the service, George was reportedly buried next to his mother Lesley in the West Cemetery at Highgate which is only accessible via paid tours – and the spot is not on the tour list so that his resting place remains private, rather than a place of pilgrimage for fans.

In the months and days before his death, George had been working on edits to Freedom, a documentary about his life. The documentary was eventually screened on Channel 4 on October 16, 2017, in a final cut almost exactly as George had left it, save a few sections added in recognition of his subsequent death.

These additions including a moving clip from an archive interview, when George had been asked about his legacy and said he'd like to be known .....'as a great singer and songwriter. I'd like to be remembered as one of the last big stars from this era of youth culture, [the era] with some glamour to it. And for having integrity.'

His integrity was in no doubt, particularly following the many stories of his incredibly generosity which emerged after his death.

Kenny Goss said that it was no exaggeration to say that George had given away more than £10 million over his lifetime. Sometimes he would make the grand gesture of a free concert for nurses, at other times, quietly and anonymously slip a cheque to someone he had heard was suffering. Richard Osman, the producer of afternoon TV show Deal or No Deal tweeted a tribute to George after he'd died saying that having heard a contestant say she needed money for IVF, George had sent in the money after the show.

'Money did not mean a lot to him', said Kenny. 'He was a very generous guy and gave money away, usually secretly.'

Despite being one of the most successful pop stars in a

generation, George believed he paid a price for the privilege of stardom and success. Instead of coming to terms with international fame, George found that the longer his fame lasted, the stranger his life became.

'If I was not driven and didn't find it impossible to live without my music in my life I wouldn't be doing this', he said in 2011.

'I haven't been happy with fame since I was 22, right. So I wished I was someone else since I was 22 because I do ... I hate the effect it has on friendships, on relationships, on your privacy. I hate it ... all of it!

'But I love the fact that I've been given the ability to make music. And I'm a kind of slave to that and I think I tried to manoeuvre emotionally through the difficulties as best I can. But I am my mother's son in that privacy would be everything to me.

'I think the way I've been treated as a gay man by the media is absolutely despicable. And I think their treatment of me has been a negative to young gay people to look at the fact that you can be so successful and still be reduced to your sexuality'.

The last word on George has to go to his friend and musical partner Andrew Ridgeley, who while paying tribute to George at the 2017 Brit awards, said;

'His is a legacy of unquestionable brilliance which will continue to shine and resonate for generations to come. George has left in his songs, in the transcendent beauty of his voice, and in the poetic expression of his soul, the very best of himself. I loved him, and in turn we, you, have been loved.'

98

DISCOGRAPHY

STUDIO ALBUMS

Faith
Listen Without Prejudice Vol. 1
Older
Songs From The Last Century
Patience

LIVE ALBUMS

Five Live
MTV Unplugged
Symphonica (2014)

COMPILATION ALBUMS

Ladies and Gentlemen – The Best of George Michael
Twenty Five

With thanks to Huw, Georgia, Francesca and Ethan
for their encouragement

ABOUT THE AUTHOR

Carolyn McHugh is an editor and author based in Southampton, England, who has written several books on musicians and rock bands. She remembers when rock was (quite) young and specialises in the sounds and culture of the 1970s and 1980s.